360

Surefire Ways to Let Your Employees Know They Count

by Carol A. Hacker

InSync
PRESS

InSync Communications LLC and InSync Press
2445 River Tree Circle
Sanford, Florida 32771
http://www.insynchronicity.com

ISBN: 1-929902-05-0
00-102072
    CIP
Hacker, Carol A., 1948-
366 Surefire Ways to Let Your Employees Know They Count

First InSync Press Edition
10 9 8 7 6 5 4 3 2

InSync Press books are available at special discounts when purchased in bulk for use in seminars, as premiums or in sales promotions. Special editions or book excerpts can also be created to specification. For details, contact InSync Communications LLC at the address above.

Cover Design by Jonathan Pennell
Book Design/Typesetting by Stephanie Murphy
Printed in the United States of America

About the Author

Carol A. Hacker is an educator, speaker, author and founder of Hacker & Associates, one of the country's foremost skill building enterprises on human resource management. For more than two decades she's been a significant voice in front-line and corporate human resource management to small businesses as well as Fortune 500 companies. With hands-on experience in managing a wide variety of public, private and non-profit projects, her client lists spans North America and Europe. Carol is the author of the highly acclaimed books, *The High Cost of Low Morale ... and what to do about it*, *The Costs of Bad Hiring Decisions & How to Avoid Them*, *Job Hunting in the 21st Century – Exploding the Myths, Exploring the Realities*, and *Hiring Top Performers – 350 Great Interview Questions For People Who Need People*.

She's an active member of National Speakers Association, Society for Human Resource Management and American Society for Training and Development. She earned her B.S. and M.S. with honors from the University of Wisconsin.

Carol draws on her strong business background to tailor management training for organizations of all types and sizes. She specializes in the areas of recruiting, retention and managing employee performance. Carol believes that the competitive strength and financial performance of any organization is directly related to the people it employs and how they're managed.

Some of her most popular workshops are:

- How to Hire Top Performers
- How to Compete in the War for Talent
- How to Take the Guesswork Out of Interviewing
- Enhancing Working Relationships
- Keeping Winners
- 21st Century Strategies for Gaining Employee Loyalty and Reducing Turnover

For more information contact:
Carol A. Hacker
209 Cutty Sark Way
Alpharetta, GA 30005
770-410-0517
CarolAHacker@hotmail.com

Dedication

To Judy L. Rogers,
my personal angel and editor.

Publisher's Note

At one time or another while on the job, we've all been treated like an endangered species of animals looking down the barrel of a disinterested and uncaring hunter's rifle. If we're honest, some people in our work lives have also treated us pretty nicely. I'm sure someone has played with the statistics and could tell us that "X" percentage of employees are treated fairly and that "Y" percentage has been treated rather shabbily.

Whatever the reality for us individually, there are a tremendous number of people in the workplace who feel as though it, "just ain't worth getting out of bed" each morning to go face a boss or manager or team member who doesn't treat you well. With unemployment at an all time low, statistically that means more people are working than ever. And with larger numbers going to work each day, chances are pretty high that many of them leave at the end of the day feeling down about their work.

Carol Hacker, a very savvy business consultant, has put together a book of ideas that are proven winners when it comes to letting employees know that they have value. Any company – no matter its size – can benefit from putting a few of these ideas to work. The results could be overwhelming – and isn't that, after all, what a productive company is looking for at the end of their respective rainbow: result?!

Motivational, invigorating, fun, outrageous, perhaps intimidating to some, the ideas contained in ***366 Surefire Ways to Let Your Employees Know They Count*** are bound to change the way your employees look at your company – and you as a leader.

366 Surefire Ways to Let Your Employees Know They Count

JANUARY

January is the start of the New Year. It's back to work after the December holidays. It's Martin Luther King, Jr.'s birthday (January 15), and it's Super Bowl month. As you kick off the New Year, try some of the following ideas to let your employees know they count.

January 1

Happy New Year! This year, acknowledge birthdays with a note of congratulations, a cake or balloon bouquet.

January 2

A ward points to employees through-out the year for attendance and individual as well as team achievements. Employees can use the points to bid on gift items at an auction held at the end of the year.

January 3

For lower wage earners with dependents, check out the advanced feature of the earned income tax credit (EIC). It requires the employee to complete a W-5 form annually. The benefit is an increase in pay without any net cost to the employee. (The extra pay is a Federal tax offset to the employee). This should be filed as close to January 1 as possible.

January 4

Start off the New Year right. Include "fun" in your company's core values that should already include respect, trust, excellence, balance, ethics, adaptability, empowerment, and risk-taking.

January 5

Provide the ingredients for "make your own" ice cream or yogurt sundaes.

January 6

Do away with performance appraisals, but give regular, verbal performance feedback.

January 7

Hold a "reverse" drawing. The last ticket called wins the grand prize; it doesn't have to be an expensive item.

January 8

Provide business cards for someone, such as a receptionist, who ordinarily wouldn't get them.

January 9

Set the coffee and soft drink vending machines on "free vend" for breaks, lunch, or even the day.

January 10

Invite employees to put their ideas about better ways to do things into an "idea book."

January 11

The "white lab coat" award: A white (or any color you choose) lab coat is awarded to the employee with the most helpful cost-saving idea of the month. The lab coat rotates every month (with laundry service provided).

January 12

Employees, or teams of employees, design crossword puzzles using industry terminology. Hold a contest to determine winners of puzzle categories, including most challenging, most typical of industry, most technical words used, most creative, and funniest.

January 13

Match your employee's monetary donation to a charitable organization and get a tax write-off as well. For example, a fisherman got the company he worked for to match his contribution to a "Fishing Has No Boundaries" program in his community.

January 14

Encourage employees to write their own job titles. One creative employee calls himself a "software gardener."

January 15
(Martin Luther King, Jr. Birthday)

Design a poster honoring an out-standing employee.

January 16

Sponsor an ice skating party at an indoor rink for employees and their family members. This is especially fun in warm climates where people don't often have the chance to ice skate.

January 17

Provide opportunities to taste the company's new products before they're introduced into the marketplace.

January 18

Name a special award (such as a safety award, production award, years of service award, community service award, or even a scholarship) after an employee.

January 19

To encourage employees to pursue charitable endeavors, give employees a certain number of paid leave hours every year to do volunteer work in the community.

January 20

Schedule a brown bag "lunch and learn" workshop on a personal development topic such as time management, diet and exercise, health, personal safety, or goal setting.

January 21

A ward U.S. Savings Bonds. There's no commission or fee and you can buy one for as little as $25.00. For questions, contact the Savings Bond Operations Office at (304) 480-6112.

January 22

Hold a picnic in the middle of winter in a snow-covered area. Play volley-ball, grill hotdogs and hamburgers and roast marshmallows.

January 23

Reduce problems with your software by holding a contest to eliminate defects. Have employees work together in teams. Award small prizes during the six-week contest. Result: reduced backlog while building team spirit. (Cost-savings more than paid for this contest.)

January 24

Surprise employees with an upgrade in computer software.

January 25

Consider paid time-off for employees who work as telephone volunteers for fund-raisers, such as charity telethons, or public television or radio events.

January 26

Make it worthwhile for employees to save their sick days. Allow them to bank sick days and use them to reduce the cost of health insurance benefits to the employee in retirement, or reduce premiums on current insurance.

January 27

L et the employee know that you're putting a note in his or her personnel file to document exceptional performance.

January 28

Hold a jeans and T-shirt day.

January 29

Lend money to employees through a formal, interest-free loan program.

January 30

It's Super Bowl month. Reward an employee(s) with two tickets to a sporting event of their choice.

January 31

Let employees bring a boom box to work and play music softly.

FEBRUARY

February presents an interesting assortment of special days that range from Groundhog Day (February 2) to Valentine's Day (February 14) to Presidents' Day (February 21) to Leap Year (February 29).
Whether you work where it's cold and snowy in February or mild and warm year around, pack some punch into February with these tips.

February 1

Include employees in a meeting they wouldn't usually attend.

February 2
(Groundhog Day)

In addition to checking on whether the groundhog sees his shadow, consider having students "shadow" mentors in the workplace. For more information, see Appendix.

February 3

Hold an "Employee Recognition" day or week. If for a week, have a small surprise each day.

February 4

Hire a graphologist to make a presentation on handwriting analysis. Give employees a chance to submit a sample of their handwriting to the instructor for feedback.

February 5

Start the day with a group sing-along.

February 6

Have employees write their own job descriptions and find out what your employees are really doing.

February 7

Sponsor a flag football game in the snow.

February 8

Present an employee with a birthday card on his or her birthday that's signed by everyone in the department.

February 9

Have a supply of postage stamps on your desk for the personal use of your employees.

February 10

Provide employees with the opportunity to cross-train in another job in another department.

February 11

Reward with a gift certificate for a free car wash and wax.

February 12

Invite employees to produce a video presentation about their department.

February 13

Help stock your community food pantry with food items or cash donations.

February 14

It's Valentine's Day. Hold a "guess the lips contest." All participants, both male and female, apply lipstick and press their lips to 3x5 cards. Cards are posted and everyone guesses which lips belong to whom.

February 15

Arrange to have a star in the galaxy named after an employee.

February 16

Sponsor a contest to design a computer-generated thank-you card for customers/clients.

February 17

Support an in-house Toastmasters Club by providing meeting space and refreshments, and/or pay a portion of the annual dues for each employee who is a member.

February 18

Surprise employees with a continental breakfast.

February 19

Collect used books and magazines for distribution to nursing homes and hospital waiting rooms.

February 20

Reward with special bonuses. It doesn't have to be a large sum of money. If it's unexpected, it's even better.

February 21

On Presidents' Day this month, invite employees to have lunch with the president in the cafeteria or break-room and ask any questions they want to ask. To eliminate fear of awkwardness, put written questions in a box to be drawn out and answered one by one until the end of the lunch break.

February 22
(Washington's Birthday)

Surprise your employees with a pancake breakfast prepared and/or served by the supervisors and managers.

February 23

Support employees in organizing an "Energizing Committee" to arrange for social events.

February 24

Help employees develop the skills needed to advance their careers.

February 25

Sponsor employees in a walk or run for charity.

February 26

Add money to an employee's retirement account.

February 27

Honor employees' special achievements using an electronic bulletin board.

February 28

Hold a "theme day" where employees can wear costumes to work.
Example: Clown Days, 50s or 60s Days, Hawaiian Days, Roaring Twenties Days, Western Days, Hobo Days, etc.

February 29

Award a gift certificate to a CD exchange store.

MARCH

According to the old saying, March "comes in like a lion and goes out like a lamb." Use these tips to get your employees to "roar" for success. Don't forget about St. Patrick's Day (March 17) and an opportunity to celebrate the wearing of the green. This is also the month when Hollywood awards Oscars—help your employees become stars in their own right.

March 1

Make it as hassle-free as possible to change jobs within the organization.

March 2

Reward top employees with the complimentary use of an income tax preparation service.

March 3

Write a personal note to employees on the back of their paycheck envelope every time they're paid. Seal with a yellow smiley face sticker.

March 4

Sponsor a forklift rodeo. If you have forklift drivers and haven't tried this safety awareness exercise, contact your truck supplier for information on how to get started.

March 5

Provide the food for "build your own sandwich" day.

March 6

Throw a "toga party."

March 7

Award gift certificates to fast food restaurants. Some restaurants will give gift certificates free of charge to employers if you ask.

March 8

Sponsor a basketball game—
employees versus their supervisors.
Everyone dresses in wild and wacky
clothing. The game is held in a company,
community or high school gymnasium
after work. Employees' families are
invited to attend along with co-workers.

March 9

Create a "walk of fame" hallway. Print the names of employees to be recognized on adhesive footprints and adhere them to the floor in a highly visible area of the company.

March 10

Keep the company refrigerator stocked with free soft drinks and juices.

March 11

Plan a "First Day of Spring" party. Springs hails the beginning of a new season of growth.

March 12

A ward compensatory time off.

March 13

Hold a monthly potluck theme lunch. Themes could be ethnic, country-western, Polynesian, low-fat, or "just salads."

March 14

Encourage your employees to practice "reach-out rituals" by keeping in touch with the elderly, or maybe volunteering for Meals on Wheels once a quarter.

March 15

A ward movie passes for the "best showing" in your business. Let employees define what the "best showing" means.

March 16

Create an "Oscar Award" with several categories. Hold an awards night with employees as the emcees. Employees might also provide entertainment between awards.

March 17

Big Foot: Everyone traces their foot on a piece of paper. Post them and hold a contest to guess which foot belongs to whom. Gag gifts may also be awarded for the longest foot, shortest foot, widest foot, narrowest foot and funniest-looking foot.

March 18

St. Patrick's Day. Greet everyone with your best Irish greeting. Put decorated cupcakes and St. Patrick's Day napkins on each employee's desk.

March 19

Give employees discounts on merchandise the company sells.

March 20

Promote from within whenever
possible.

March 21

Promote your superstars ahead of schedule.

March 22

Award with a prepaid telephone card.

March 23

Provide an assortment of picture puzzles in the employee breakroom.

March 24

Designate a "VP of Fun" or "Minister of Happiness"—a position with responsibility for leading a committee that proposes social events. Position is filled by employee vote.

March 25

Offer "English as a second language" classes on company property before and/or after work.

March 26

Have employees build a "wishing well" with all the money collected donated to charity.

March 27

When they reach a goal, surprise your employees with an extra 15-minute break.

March 28

Recognize employees for their hard work with a classified ad in the local newspaper. Consider mentioning the names of each employee in the ad. Go one step further and include a photo of the entire team along with a few words of "thanks" or congratulations.

March 29

Hire an artist for a day or a long group-lunch to draw caricatures of your employees.

March 30

Offer free haircuts, or free pedicures/manicures.

March 31

L et an employee set his or her own schedule for the week.

APRIL

This month brings the day most people dread—April 15th—the deadline for filing personal tax returns with the IRS. This is also the month when Daylight Saving Time begins and we "lose" an hour of sleep. And don't forget to honor your secretary, or the department's secretaries, on Secretary's Day.

April 1

Teach them how to juggle balls. Once they master juggling, they can become instructors. Juggling is a great metaphor for mastering a variety of tasks.

April 2

As an on-the-spot reward, tell the employee to take a break for one hour while you take over his or her job.

April 3

Send a thank-you letter to the employees' children. The text might say something like: "Please accept my sincere appreciation for the support you have given to your mother (dad) in her (his) pursuit of a career with our company. I'm fortunate to have her (him) on the team and want you to know how lucky you are to have her (him) as your parent." This letter could also be adapted for a spouse, or the spouse and children of an employee.

April 4

Hold a "Muffin Friday" every month. Employees sign up for a Friday when they will provide the muffins, sweet rolls and/or bagels for everyone. Employees arrive at work 15 minutes early to enjoy the goodies.

April 5

Designate a wall or area where employees can exhibit their artwork or craft work for all to admire.

April 6

Award a gift certificate for a one-time housecleaning by a professional service.

April 7

Hold a kite-flying contest with categories such as the highest flying, most colorful, most unusual, longest in the air, and a booby prize for the first to crash.

April 8

Greet all employees with a smile and call them by name.

April 9

Give the gift of personalized stationery or note cards.

April 10

Create a lending library. Employees and the company donate books to the employee-run library.

April 11

Award the executive privilege of an extra 15 minutes for lunch.

April 12

Provide space for employees to set up and grow herbs and spices year-round.

April 13

Have an on-site blood drive. Coordinate this with your community blood bank. Consider giving employees who donate blood one-half day off with pay.

April 14

Dedicate special parking places for peak performers based on measurable accomplishments. Rotate monthly or quarterly.

April 15

I f you supervise the finance
department, hold an April 15th or end
of the corporate fiscal year celebration as
a reward for all their hard work.

April 16

Hold an employee talent show. Sometimes they're more of a Gong Show, but they're fun.

April 17

Send a postcard to the employee when you're out of town on business. Example: "John—Thank you for your support. Does this picture look like a market opportunity? With your help, they'll all be our customers too."

April 18

Reward with a three-day weekend with the third day paid. Consider this idea for acknowledging your secretary's hard work.

April 19

Provide an all-expense-paid trip for an employee to the annual shareholders' meeting.

April 20

Keep employees involved with the business at hand. Use adhesive foil stars at staff meetings as recognition. When someone offers a helpful suggestion, gets everyone laughing, or shares an interesting thought, anyone at the meeting may award that person with a star. An individual may also award him- or herself with a star.

April 21

Reward an employee with an opportunity to be in a company radio or television commercial, or at least to observe the recording or filming of the commercial.

April 22

Establish an "ugly tie rack." Place a sign on it that says: "Going to a job interview? Meeting with the boss? Borrow one of these if you need to."

April 23

Establish a hotline so employees can share their hottest ideas. Record their messages so that everyone can access all the ideas at any time.

April 24

Establish a mentor program. Match an entry-level manager with a higher level professional. All mentors must be volunteers because someone who is "required" to participate is usually not effective.

April 25

Offer "casual days for charity." Employees pay to wear shorts or jeans to work for a specific period of time and the money goes to charity.

April 26

Each month, provide bagels, donuts and coffee or tea for all employees on the teams that reach their goals.

April 27

Hold periodic standing ovations to recognize special achievements.

April 28

Provide space for employees to plant and oversee gardens on company property. For example, one company provides space on the roof of their building.

April 29

Offer a free weekend or week in a company-owned timeshare.

April 30

For the business traveler, reward with an upgrade from a hotel room to a suite.

MAY

Spring is in full bloom by now, so use some of these tips to keep your employees from suffering "spring fever." Special days this month include Mother's Day, Armed Forces Day and Memorial Day. May is also graduation month for many colleges.

May 1

Re-deploy employees from downsized departments to expanding areas of the company rather than terminate their employment.

May 2

Award a gift certificate for dry-cleaning.

May 3

Thank employees for their efforts in front of their peers.

May 4

Invite employees to bring their baby pictures to display. Everyone tries to guess who they are. The employee with the most correct guesses gets a baby bottle, pacifier or rattle.

May 5

Throw a mystery lunch party. Teams of employees have the fun of solving a mystery similar to that done in a mystery dinner theater.

May 6

Provide money for on-the-spot financial rewards whereby an employee can honor a co-worker for doing something that deserves special recognition.

May 7

Invite employees to share a hobby or special interest on a "show and tell" day.

May 8

Recognize employees when they receive their GED, high school diploma, college degree, or a special certificate or license such as CPA.

May 9

Set up a complimentary gourmet coffee and tea station.

May 10

After 60 days of employment, top performers earn the use of a house charge account for business expenses.

May 11

Reward employees with cards and small gift items from a store that offers motivational products, such as Successories.®

May 12

Invite employees to submit their favorite recipes for inclusion in a company cookbook.

May 13

Sponsor a food/clothing drive for the homeless.

May 14

Pay for one week of childcare.

May 15

Send flowers or a gift certificate to the employee's spouse.

May 16

Arrange for a surprise picnic in the company parking lot.

May 17

Invite employees to participate in a new-hire orientation by explaining what goes on in their departments.

May 18

Surprise employees with free drink tickets for airline flights.

May 19

Be a corporate sponsor of a foreign exchange student.

May 20

Pass out "Kudo"® candy bars for a job well done.

May 21

Reward a group of employees (and/or their children) with the opportunity to ride on a company float in a community parade.

May 22

Is your team going to a meeting or holding a special event? Try this as a warm-up. Select one individual to be the "clue master." Several days before the event is to take place, have each of the event participants send an e-mail to the "clue master" with a fact about themselves. This could be a past life event, a previous job, or an interesting hobby. Facts are compiled and associated with each participant by the "clue master." At the event all participants receive (at the same time) a listing of all the facts. As participants mingle they search to match facts with other individual participants. Participants should be cagey about giving up clues about their fact. At a prescribed time the search stops. The person with the most correct answers wins the "Sherlock

Holmes" prize, awarded by the "clue master."

May 23

Set up table tennis or pool tables for employees to enjoy before and after work or during breaks.

May 24

Hold an office clean-up day. Everyone is dedicated to cleaning up their workspace as well as the common area. Celebrate afterwards with a luncheon for all.

May 25

Volunteers are needed at Ronald McDonald Houses. (See Appendix for details.) Offer employees time off twice a year to help out, or allow employees to earn one hour of personal time for each day volunteered.

May 26

Reward employees with an extra day of vacation.

May 27

Name a product you manufacture after an employee who has had a significant achievement.

May 28

Manager does a "happy dance" dressed in an outrageous costume to celebrate a major achievement by the team.

May 29

Give a bookstore gift certificate.

May 30
(Memorial Day)

Provide a meal when employees volunteer to work overtime or on a holiday.

May 31

Hold a bake-off with specific categories such as brownies, breads, cakes, pies and cookies.

JUNE

June marks the beginning of the summer months. School is out and employees begin to think about vacation and fun times. Keep their attention focused at work with these ideas. Special days this month include Flag Day and Father's Day.

June 1

Hold an outrageous hairstyle or junky jewelry day.

June 2

Award a free round of golf with the company president at his or her country club.

June 3

Recognize an employee for a "life saving" idea with a necklace made from Lifesavers®.

June 4

Get to work before your employees arrive and leave small surprises such as a candy bar, key chain, company identified merchandise in the form of caps or T-shirts in each employee's work area.

June 5

Have the managers wash the employees' cars.

June 6

Take a break with your team for an off-site meeting and social time.

June 7

Hold a contest to guess the date when the temperature first reaches 80 degrees.

June 8

Pin or tape paper streamers to the ceiling of the office or plant to recognize and celebrate each goal the team reaches.

June 9

In a printing firm: employees get anything they want printed for free as long as it's for personal use.

June 10

Offer telecommuting. However, it needs a formal, written policy and support from upper management to make the difference between a commitment to working out the kinks or a transfer back to the office.

June 11

Give employees a day off with pay for their birthdays.

June 12

Sponsor employees in foot races, walkathons, marathons or triathlons. Employees get a free T-shirt and the company helps build camaraderie.

June 13

Donate money to public television in the name of your employees.

June 14
(Flag Day)

Place a miniature American flag on each employee's desk. Hold a contest to see how many employees can name all 50 states within a specified period of time. Winner(s) gets an extra 30 minutes for lunch.

June 15

When an employee earns a patent, put the first page of the patent on a plaque and present it to the employee in a ceremony in front of his or her peers.

June 16

Take employees on a go-cart outing.

June 17

Invite employees to participate in a company-paid, off-site seminar.

June 18

Surprise employees with an airline ticket upgrade.

June 19

Allow employees to repair computers on company time, up to a certain limit. Donate computers to local schools.

June 20

Hold a hallway golf tournament in the office or plant. Let the employees build the course, but only with items that are already somewhere in the company. They may not bring anything from home.

June 21

Award a month's supply of food for the employee's pet.

June 22

Provide picnic tables for employees so they can eat outside in warm weather.

June 23

Make a quotation book. When employees say something noteworthy, hear something they want to remember, or read an interesting quote, enter it into the book to share with all.

June 24

Sponsor a "walk a mile in my shoes" day. Employees in various departments within the company get to experience firsthand what day-to-day activities keep their co-workers challenged. The goal is to increase respect among co-workers while promoting company awareness.

June 25

Hold a bake sale or other fund-raiser for an employee or an employee's family member with extraordinary medical or living expenses because of illness.

June 26

Set an aggressive time line for work so that there's scheduled time for officially sanctioned fun.

June 27

Recognize those who volunteer in their community with a Community Service Award.

June 28

Take employees on a nature walk. You may be surprised how much people know and are eager to share about their environment.

June 29

Offer 10-minute neck and shoulder massages on-site on company time. Have employees sign up in advance.

June 30

Reward new employees who stick with you for a specified period of time (six months or more) with a pair of Nike® shoes. This reward is particularly popular with teens and young adults in the hospitality industry where turnover is traditionally high.

JULY

The beginning of July means we're halfway through the year. Celebrate Independence Day this month not only with a day off but with some fun at the workplace. Don't let the July heat wilt your employees' energy and enthusiasm. Keep them excited about working for you with the following tips.

July 1

Provide a suggestion box. Implement the most valuable suggestions. However, be sure to let your employees know you consider *all* of their ideas.

July 2

Award employees with portable hand-tools, such as an electric drill, power screwdriver, Skil® saw, wrench or socket set.

July 3

Recognize the diversity that your employees bring to the workplace. Glue a large map of the world on bulletin board material and hang it on the wall. Employees who have lived in a country other than the United States get to put a long pin on the city in the country where they lived.

July 4
(Independence Day)

Hold a beer-tasting party. Admission is a six-pack of fine microbrewery beer per person or couple. The company provides the meeting place and the snacks. Feature a knowledgeable microbrewery brew-master as a speaker.

July 5

Have each department host an open house. All employees of the company are invited to attend. Serve coffee and cake or snacks and soft drinks to the guests.

July 6

A llow an employee the privilege of flexing his or her work schedule for a specified amount of time.

July 7

Hold a pet photo contest. Judge photos in different categories such as most unusual pet, largest and smallest pet, most animated face, or even the pet that looks most like its owner.

July 8

Throw a party to celebrate when an employee becomes a U.S. citizen.

July 9

Provide free or discounted passes for public transportation.

July 10

Have each team give themselves a name and create and display a coat of arms that represents every member of the team.

July 11

R eward the employee with a personalized vehicle license plate.

July 12

A team collectively writes a poem about the work they're doing or on any subject related to who they are and their roles in the company.

July 13

Adopt a highway. Take your team on a Saturday to clean up a stretch of highway near the work site or any place in the community that needs help. Provide refreshments.

July 14

Let an employee use your vehicle or boat for a day.

July 15

Name a menu item in the company cafeteria in honor of an employee.

July 16

Planning an outside event in a park? Try Frisbee® golf. Set up a nine-hole course using large plastic laundry baskets that are numbered according to hole. Print score cards with a layout of the course. Rules of golf apply.

July 17

Hold a family day when each employee may bring a child to work to see what his or her parent does for a living.

July 18

When employees are moved to a new area, i.e., department moves to a new floor/building, have balloon(s) tied to a bag of candy/cookies at each desk.

July 19

Some progressive nursing homes allow visiting pets as a way to boost life interest among residents. Sponsor a "take your pet to visit senior citizens" day. This could be a regular, on-going program throughout the year or a one-time event.

July 20

Decorate his or her work area on the employee's birthday. The entire team may want to get involved in creating this birthday fun-day.

July 21

If you believe your employees "work hard" so they can "play hard," why not offer an extra week of paid vacation immediately?

July 22

Hold a "snow day" in the middle of summer or in a warm climate where it never snows. A company in South Florida did. Requires acquiring snow or making your own.

July 23

Celebrate with a Founder's Day breakfast or lunch.

July 24

If your company is listed on the stock exchange, hold "stock watch" meetings. It's a great motivator when employees gather to discuss how the stock is doing, especially if the company is doing well. Even when it's not, it's a time to get together and discuss what the company/department is doing to reach its goals.

July 25

Promote a drive to collect used eyeglasses. Donate them to the local Lions Club for recycling.

July 26

Offer the executive privilege of arriving at work five minutes late and leaving five minutes early.

July 27

Send a memo to the employee's supervisor's supervisor about the great job the employee is doing.

July 28

Hold a "catch and release" fishing contest with prizes given for the person who catches the first fish, largest fish, smallest fish, most colorful fish and most unusual fish.

July 29

If your employees must pay for parking, provide an opportunity to earn free parking. It's a great way to give them a raise.

July 30

Provide a "pull board." For every 150 contracts keyed, or telephone calls answered, employees get to pull one ticket off the board. They can exchange tickets for prizes or cash awards.

July 31

Take your employees to a virtual reality club for an afternoon or evening of fun.

AUGUST

The summer is almost over. If you have had summer interns or student employees, now is the time to acknowledge their efforts before they return to school, especially if you want them back next summer.

August 1

Invite a competent employee to write a set of instructions or a standard operating procedure.

August 2

Recognize temporary employees with a framed certificate thanking them for their contributions to the company.

August 3

Vote for "Employee of the Month." Let each employee have two votes so they can vote once for themselves if they choose to do so.

August 4

Encourage arriving-on-time to staff meetings by asking the latest arrival to provide snacks for the next meeting. If everyone is on time, the manager or next most senior-ranking person buys for the next meeting.

August 5

Provide space for a company band or chorus to practice.

August 6

Implement a "Star of the Month" award where employees vote for the individual who went the extra mile for a co-worker or customer.

August 7

Send employees on a scavenger hunt on company property or to an off-site location. Provide each team with a disposable camera to photograph the items they find that are on the list. Have the film developed within one hour while employees share tales of the fun of the adventure.

August 8

Make a donation to the Humane Society in the name of the employee's pet(s). Preferably the pet is not deceased!

August 9

Provide a reserved parking space at the airport "Park 'n Ride" so the employee always has a convenient place to park.

August 10

Invite employees to participate in a company focus group regarding new products or a subject of concern or interest to everyone.

August 11

Anonymously, have a pizza, cake, balloons or flowers delivered to an employee or team of employees for reaching a significant goal.

August 12

Take employees to an indoor "rock-climbing" facility. Take turns climbing the "rock" blindfolded while a partner calls out directions. It's fun and a great team-building exercise.

August 13

Sponsor a foster child in a third-world country and challenge the other departments in the company to do the same.

August 14

Transfer or purchase frequent flyer points for an employee's account.

August 15

Throw a surprise "this is your life" party for the employee(s) in recognition of special achievements, retirement, or just for fun.

August 16

Sponsor a paper-airplane-flying contest.

August 17

Have a "wish list" whereby employees can fill out what they want their next week's work schedule to look like. Supervisors try to honor requests as much as possible. This is especially useful in the hospitality industry.

August 18

When the company upgrades its computer hardware and software, offer the old equipment and software to employees at nominal cost for home use.

August 19

Donate 2-5% of your profits to non-profit organizations in your community. If you're a retailer, place a sticker on selected merchandise that will support a given charity.

August 20

Recognize an employee by having the company cafeteria prepare a favorite recipe provided by the employee.

August 21

Reward employees by inviting them to attend a national sales meeting or conference with their manager.

August 22

Take your employees on a rafting or tubing trip on a hot summer day.

August 23

L end a bouquet of flowers: Bring a bouquet of flowers to work and give it to an employee with instructions to keep and enjoy it for 30 minutes (or one hour), then pass it on to another employee with the same instructions.

August 24

Stretch assignments for hi-potential employees. People who feel challenged are more likely to stay with you and grow with the company.

August 25

Hold a silent auction for charity. Donated items may be new or used.

August 26

Offer a variety of books from which an employee may select and keep a book as a reward for good work.

August 27

Australian Body Works of Atlanta, a health club, offers a "Spot an Eagle in Flight" award. "Eagle of the Moment" is a program that allows their members to recognize employees. Cards are available to fill out and turn in to the Member Services desk when a member spots an "eagle in flight."

August 28

Set up a swap-shop on a Saturday or a swap-board at the office for employees to buy and sell sports equipment or other pre-owned items.

August 29

Implement "no-pay-day" paydays. On the week that employees don't receive a paycheck, hold drawings for small prizes.

August 30

R eward with lottery tickets.

August 31

Hold a "Who Can Dress in the Most Colors Day?"

SEPTEMBER

The first Monday in September is Labor Day. Do something special this month to tell your employees how much you value their efforts and appreciate their work. September also marks the beginning of a new school year which may impact the lives of employees with children, as they adjust to a more hectic schedule.

September 1

Provide in-house instructors or pay tuition for employees to attend school to get their GEDs.

September 2

Award gift certificates for $5 through $25 in a drawing for employees who have perfect attendance for the month.

September 3

Consider the "I'll Find a Way" recognition program. Employees share stories in staff meetings about co-workers who have gone out of their way for customers.

September 4

Have each department develop a theme game. Example: During Hospital Week, "guess how many syringes are in the jar" was a game one hospital department created, to the delight of their co-workers.

September 5

Invite employees to wear their school or favorite team colors to work to kick-off the football season.

September 6

Reward with software for an employee's home computer.

September 7

Throw a bowling party and invite employees and their families to bowl or simply relax and watch.

September 8

Recognize the most energetic employee of the month in front of his or her peers with an Energizer® battery.

September 9

Offer full or partial scholarships to employees' children.

September 10

Be sensitive to family issues. Show flexibility when an employee needs time off to attend a child's school or sporting event. Make concessions as needed for people without children, too. You'll find this idea to be an incentive for growth and long-term employment.

September 11

Award with a "Scratch and Win" card of company design. Employees scratch off the company logo and win one of many small gift items such as a soft drink, a bag of chips, a candy bar, pack of gum, or any typical vending machine item. The dollar value of the item isn't important; it's the fun of scratching and winning that employees enjoy.

September 12

Hold a company-wide Olympic event.
Employees compete in running, hurdles,
cross-country, discus throw, etc.

September 13

Arrange for a company representative to participate in a high school career fair or to speak in a classroom of an employee's child.

September 14

Reward employees with a personalized pair of Levi® jeans. For $55, consumers can design jeans with the precise Levi's models, leg openings, colors, sizes, zippers or buttons they want. Orders are usually filled within two weeks.

September 15

Have the president or a high-ranking member of the company telephone an employee in your department and thank him or her for a particularly outstanding accomplishment.

September 16

Turn the break-room or cafeteria into a "cruise ship" with island decor, fruit punch, buffet lunch, and the aroma of suntan oil.

September 17

Delegate whenever possible. If you're not comfortable with delegating, make an effort to learn how. It's another way of letting your employees know that you trust them, as well as getting the work done.

September 18

Provide free microwave popcorn and a microwave oven in which to pop it.

September 19

Arrange for employees to appear on a local telethon to present a monetary gift on behalf of the company and its employees to a charity such as one that conducts medical research on muscular dystrophy, cerebral palsy, multiple sclerosis, heart disease or cancer.

September 20

Support a "Roving Recognition Band" as does Tricon Global Restaurants, Inc., in Louisville, Kentucky. Kazoos buzz, plastic noisemakers shriek and cowbells clang to shatter an early morning calm at corporate headquarters. Band employees, in casual dress, drop in on other employees they've been told deserve an extra pat on the back for a great job. The band is one method they use to "rev up" their 750,000 employees.

September 21

Contribute toward the cost of tutoring services for employees who have children with special needs.

September 22

Throw a pizza-and-a-cartoon party. Employees can watch cartoons during lunch and enjoy pizza paid for by the company.

September 23

The entire department takes a new employee to lunch on his or her first day at work, just as is often done when someone leaves. What better way to help make the new employee feel welcome and give him or her a chance to get to know the rest of the team?

September 24

Offer continuous training and development opportunities. Don't be like the manager who said he didn't want his people trained because once trained, he lost them to his competition. Ignorance is a high price to pay. Encourage your employees to grow by offering on-going learning opportunities.

September 25

Support employees that volunteer to prepare and serve meals in a homeless shelter.

September 26

Award an on-line gift certificate. For example, the on-line book retailer www.amazon.com issues gift certificates through its Web site. Another Website is www.webcertificate.com. Select the denomination, choose a design and include a personal message. Then send the certificate instantly over the

Internet. The recipient can spend it at one or several on-line stores until the credit limit is depleted. Be aware of expiration dates on all gift certificates.

September 27

Pay for the initial membership fee and first month's membership dues to a local health club.

September 28

Sponsor bowling, golf, softball, soccer and other team or league events.

September 29

Offer "VIC" days—a combination of vacation and sick days that employees may take with no questions asked.

September 30

Pay for a professional association magazine subscription.

OCTOBER

October brings not only Columbus Day (10th) and the World Series, but the end of Daylight Savings Time and Halloween on the 31st. This month also usually brings cooler weather. Use these tips to keep your employees excited about working with you.

October 1

Set a good example. You can expect no more from those who work for you than you're willing to give yourself.

October 2

Award an automobile CD player.

October 3

Recognize new employees by painting their names on coffee mugs. Have the mugs waiting for them on their desks on the day they start work.

October 4

If you're the manager, just for fun wear a baseball uniform and cap and pass out popcorn at a staff meeting.

October 5

Sponsor a flag football team. Provide logo T-shirts for each team member.

October 6

Throw a party for everyone who retires. Also, consider sponsoring a retirees club that meets monthly.

October 7

If you hear someone yell "bingo" while you're taking an order, it's not because of the total you just rang up. It's phone reps who answer the telephone playing "states bingo" while they punch in sales orders.

October 8

Hold monthly anniversary lunches where everyone hired during that month is recognized for his or her contribution to the organization.

October 9

Offer free flu shots.

October 10
(Columbus Day)

Celebrate success. Everyone wants to work for a winning company. Applaud the achievements of your employees. Don't dwell on what hasn't happened; you can't change the past. Learn from both your mistakes and your successes and move on.

October 11

You can "lend" an employee to the United Way for the period of their fund-raising campaign in your community.

October 12

Set up a weaving loom that employees can collectively work on at their leisure to create a company wall hanging.

October 13

Plan to collect toys for "Toys for Tots."
See Appendix for information.

October 14

Keep top performers under constant review to be sure they're being rewarded and provided with plenty of training and development opportunities.

October 15

Welcome new hires by being prepared for their first day on the job. Make sure the workspace has office supplies, software loaded on their computers, and a nameplate placed on their desks. Show them restrooms, breakrooms, the cafeteria and how to use the telephone features. Don't assume someone else has taken care of these things. Helping new employees get off on the right foot is critical to keeping them for the long haul.

October 16

Hold a pumpkin-decorating contest—no carving, just drawing, dressing, etc. Or hold a carving contest if you prefer.

October 17

Provide a broad experience base of rotational assignments. Most people like variety. Give employees a chance to find out what it's like to work on different assignments in different parts of the organization.

October 18

If you have college students working for you, pay to have a term paper typed for them.

October 19

Hold a drive to collect used bicycles for needy kids at Christmas. Bikes are repaired and/or cleaned by employees before distribution to charities. Get started in Fall.

October 20

Kitchen staff needs recognition too. One hotel gives out "Golden Knife" awards for exemplary performance over a specified period of time. The knife is made of fancy steel and brass and engraved with the employee's name and time period of award (in this case, monthly). The knives are displayed in a trophy case adjacent to the restaurant.

October 21

Offer the opportunity to job-share as a reward for good performance.

October 22

Employees dress in Halloween costumes and each department builds a haunted house. The children of employees are invited to trick-or-treat and visit the haunted houses from 5-7pm.

October 23

If you're redesigning the workspace, get employees involved in the actual design as well as selection of furniture, flooring covering, and wall color. Make the final result a team effort.

October 24

Learn to give feedback without causing defensiveness. Everyone benefits when feedback is given in the helping spirit. Learn how to do this and your employees will have reason to grow with the company because they know you have their best interests in mind when offering criticism.

October 25

Plan to hold a Halloween costume contest on the 31st. Make it a theme party where everyone dresses like a storybook character or favorite celebrity.

October 26

Reward with karate, skating, skiing, golfing or dance lessons for employees or their children.

October 27

ProTech Publishing and Communications, Inc. in New Albany, Indiana, holds a "Are You a Pizza Giraffe?" recognition award for people who help those in need in the community. Example: Employee earns money for a local charity by sponsoring a Special Olympics team, or raises awareness for a particular cause. Pizza Giraffes, those who go the extra mile, are regularly featured in their industry magazine, *Pizza Today*. Magazine subscribers, most of whom are pizza operators, make the nominations.

October 28

Hold a contest to guess the date of the first snowfall.

October 29

Offer a coupon for a free lunch in the company cafeteria.

October 30

Give the "Diaper Award" (a diaper with the company logo on it) to new parents.

October 31

Invite employees to bring old ties and scarves to work and use them to make a piece of "modern art."

NOVEMBER

Help your employees be "thankful" this month: acknowledge, praise and reward their efforts. Special events this month include Veterans Day (November 11) and Thanksgiving Day.

November 1

Designate a wall as the "Employee Wall of Fame." Post customer appreciation letters that recognize your employees for a great job or for going out of their way to serve a customer.

November 2

During the holidays, reward employees with "Holly Money" that can be used to purchase company-identified merchandise or items in the company store, restaurant, or hotel.

November 3

Have the CEO send a personalized note to a new employee at the end of his or her first week on the job.

November 4

Hold a Harvest Ball in November and invite employees to come to work in old bridesmaid dresses and tuxedos.

November 5

Hold a hot soup slow-cooker party. Each employee who chooses to participate contributes one can or package of soup. All soups are mixed together for a wonderful potpourri of flavors. Serve with breads and beverages provided by the company.

November 6

G ive the gift of time with a watch;
consider a sports watch with the
company logo or a motivational message
on the face of the watch.

November 7

If it's an election year, on Election Day give employees time off to vote.

November 8

Refer to all employees as "associates" rather than "employees."

November 9

Give gift certificates for food at Thanksgiving or Christmas instead of a turkey or ham. Employees may then purchase what they want, not what the company thinks they want.

November 10

Focus on the results, not the rules. Don't punish employees by constantly reminding them about the rules and regulations. The results of their efforts are usually more important than how they reached their goals.

November 11
(Veterans Day)

Pay for one month of elder care services for an employee's family member.

November 12

Employees nominate and vote for "supervisor of the year."

November 13

Encourage your team of employees to become "bell ringers" for the Salvation Army during the Christmas holidays.

November 14

Arrange for an executive level employee to spend one-half day with an employee doing the employee's job.

November 15

Celebrate moments of success using confetti and horns. Employees "hoot and holler" for 60 seconds in recognition of their team's accomplishments.

November 16

Take your employees bowling for Thanksgiving using frozen 10 to 20 pound turkeys as bowling balls. The winners get fresh turkeys to take home.

November 17

Promote new responsibilities, not promotions. There are times when there is no place to be "promoted to" in an organization. That's the time to take this idea to heart and get creative.

November 18

Surprise your managers with a limousine to pick them up and take them to an off-site meeting.

November 19

Make tabletop holiday decorations for nursing home residents.

November 20

After an especially busy week, to recognize extra effort put Hershey Kisses® on everyone's desk before they arrive at work on Friday morning.

November 21

Pay for dues in a professional association.

November 22

Hold a progressive lunch. The employees provide the food. Start in one department with hors d'oeuvres, progress to the next department for soup or salad, the next department for the main course and the last department for dessert.

November 23

Send a team photograph with the words, "We proudly made this product," with every shipment the company makes.

November 24

Offer career and expectation planning sessions. Even if your organization doesn't offer a formal program of this type, don't let it stop you from talking to your employees about their future plans.

November 25

If you own a restaurant, once a month invite the employee and his or her family for dinner in appreciation for excellent work.

November 26

Arrange for an employee to spend a day with a sales representative. It's a great way to show appreciation as well as give the employee a chance to learn more about the business.

November 27

Schedule a 5-minute break during which everyone says something nice to a co-worker.

November 28

Hold a "polka dot" day. Everyone dresses in polka dots. Give a prize for the person wearing the most dots.

November 29

In snow country, offer a ski-slope pass for a day.

November 30

Allow a star salesperson the privilege of not having to schedule any outside appointments for a day.

DECEMBER

Employees may have their minds on the upcoming holidays this month. This is an excellent time to encourage camaraderie among team members, demonstrate concern for others, and prepare for the New Year. Special days this month include Hanukkah, Christmas and New Year's Eve. Wind up the year with these tips that will help everyone enjoy the holiday spirit.

December 1

If you own a restaurant, once a month invite the employee and his or her family for dinner in appreciation for excellent work.

December 2

Consider an American Express Gift Cheque. It's a gift certificate that can be used almost anywhere. The checks are available in $25, $50 and $100 denominations, and come in a gold envelope with a gift card. There's a $2.50 charge for each check, regardless of denomination. They're replaceable if lost or stolen. You can buy American Express Gift Cheques at many banks, or by calling (800) 828-4438.

December 3

Set up a hobby room with basic equipment (workbenches, vices, and simple tools) and hold weekend or after-hours classes taught by volunteer employee-instructors.

December 4

Provide games (backgammon, chess, checkers, Monopoly® and cribbage) in breakrooms for employees to enjoy during their free time.

December 5

Managers: Share your perks, such as tickets for sporting events, fruit baskets and other gifts managers frequently receive, especially during the holidays. The people who work for you are often aware of such gifts even though you may not think so. Why not allow others to enjoy them too?

December 6

Hold an end-of-year auction where employees use the award points (see tip for January 2) they've collected throughout the year to bid on gift items.

December 7

Hold a Christmas tree ornament exchange.

December 8

Name conference rooms after long-term employees. The nameplate remains above the door of the room until the employee retires.

December 9

Provide fresh fruit once a month for employees to enjoy at work.

December 10

Invite an employee to conduct a staff meeting in your absence.

December 11

Offer a modified sabbatical where a modest amount of money is paid to the employee and/or insurance premium is paid in full while he or she is on a leave of absence.

December 12

Hold a cookie swap. Each employee who participates brings one dozen cookies to exchange. Everyone leaves with a variety of holiday treats.

December 13

Sponsor a white elephant gift exchange in lieu of holiday gift-giving. Money that would have been spent on purchased gifts goes to charity.

December 14

Have fruit, chocolate, nuts, jellies or jams delivered monthly to an employee's home for a specified period of time.

December 15

Humanize the workplace by hiring people-oriented leaders. People who care about other people are the most likely to be successful in managing the work of others.

December 16

Have an "Ugliest Christmas Tree Ornament" contest. Employees vote for the winning ornament. The winner gets a $10 gift certificate.

December 17

Support a writers' club both for employees who aspire to write as well as published authors.

December 18

Give delivery drivers who use their own vehicles a free oil change or a free tank of gas.

December 19

Collect used greeting cards for St. Jude's Born Again Recycling Program. (See Appendix for information.)

December 20

Write a year-end letter to your employees, sharing the department's successes for the year. Include something about everyone on the team. Part of the text might say: "Let me express my sincere thanks to the entire team for the dedicated and skilled work that was performed throughout the year. We couldn't have reached our goal without everyone's help. Here are some examples of your major accomplishments...."

December 21

Award "gift selector catalogs."
Catalogs can be given for increased
production, sales contests, perfect
attendance, service awards, retirement
gifts, safety awards, or employee of the
month. Employees can select from many
gift items featured in the catalogs.

December 22

Form a bingo club. Employees play bingo at lunch during the winter months. Award $5 bills to the winners.

December 23

Secret Pal: Each employee draws a name and that employee then becomes his or her secret pal for 3 months to one year. Throughout that time period pals surprise each other on birthdays, anniversaries with the company, and for no reason at all with a

card or small gift. Hold a company
function at the end of the year (or
sooner) where secret pals reveal their
identity to each other.

December 24

R eward with a gift card, such as that offered by First USA. The plastic, prepaid cards are available in any amount, starting at $50.00. Each time the recipient uses the card, the purchase amount is deducted from it. The cards come in 11 designs and bear the recipient's name and a personal greeting of up to 19 characters. They can be used anywhere a VISA credit card is accepted. To order, call: (888) 378-4438.

December 25
(Christmas Day)

Consider a donation to Los Medicos Voladores (LMV), also known as the "Flying Doctors." (See Appendix for information.)

December 26

Pay for a one-time grooming of the employee's pet.

December 27

Save old calendar pages from desk top calendars such as Gary Larson's "Far Side" or John Gray's "Men are from Mars, Women are from Venus." When writing a note of appreciation to an employee, write it on one of the calendar pages that comes closest to fitting the occasion.

December 28

Designate a wall as "The Wall of the Absurd." Invite employees to post funny or absurd cartoons, quotes, actual memos, media articles, or jokes, as long as they are not offensive in nature. You may want to have an employee committee approve postings on a weekly basis.

December 29

Hold a "wellness day" and offer free blood pressure and cholesterol checks along with literature on health-related topics.

December 30

Award all employees a specific amount of "well" days in lieu of "sick" days.

December 31

Award a gift certificate for a facial or color analysis.

APPENDIX

February 2

Groundhog ,Job Shadow Day: In February 2000, half a million students across America were paired with workplace mentors as part of a nationwide initiative called Groundhog Job Shadow Day. The idea is for students to spend half a day in a mentored work site shadowing an employee as he or she goes through a normal day on the job. In 1998 on Groundhog Job Shadow Day, close to 400 students in three states shadowed employees in restaurants and hotels. In 1999, the National Restaurant Association joined forces with the American Hotel & Motel Association and the Hospitality Business Alliance to get students involved in shadowing employees in restaurants and hotels in all

50 states. Call (800) 424-5156, ext. 3679. Groundhog Job Shadow Day is a joint effort of America's Promise (headed by General Colin Powell), the American Society of Association Executives, Junior Achievement, and the National School-to-Work Office.

May 25

Ronald McDonald House volunteers: Volunteers are needed at Ronald McDonald Houses to answer phones, talk with parents, work on projects with staff members, or comfort a child. They also need people to help produce the major house events like golf and tennis tournaments, or help wrap gifts for donations during the holidays. Supper volunteers provide and coordinate a meal. Garden volunteers maintain the grounds at the Ronald McDonald House. Other volunteers provide such services as leading art projects, presenting plays for children, or helping with sing-alongs. Call the Ronald McDonald House at 708-575-7418 or Ronald McDonald Children's Charity at 708-575-7048.

October 13

Toys for Tots: The U.S. Marine Corps Reserve Toys for Tots Program is directed by the Commander, Marine Forces Reserve, and his staff from the Marine Forces Reserve Headquarters in New Orleans, Louisiana. The Commander, Marine Forces Reserve, has under his command 187 Marine Corps Reserve Units located in 46 states, the District of

Columbia, and Puerto Rico. Each Reserve Unit and approved MCL Detachment conduct toy collection and distribution campaigns in the communities surrounding their Reserve Center of Detachment headquarters each year. Campaigns begin in October and last until December 22nd. Local business leaders play a key role by allowing Marines to locate collection receptacles in their stores. Businesses provide free warehouse space during October, November and December for storing and sorting toys. They also provide vehicles in which to collect toys from collection sites, sponsor toy and fund-raising events, and help Marines receive maximum media exposure for Toys for Tots. For more information on how you can help, call (703) 640-9433.

December 19

St. Jude's Born Again Recycling
Program: St. Jude's Ranch for Children
is a Nevada community focusing on the
needs of abused, abandoned and
neglected children of all races and faiths.
Children take the front of greeting cards
of all occasions (not limited to
Christmas), glue them to preprinted card
backs and sell the "new" cards to the

public. Donors should send card fronts only, with no writing on the reverse and that can be trimmed to fit 5-by-7-inch card backs. Send to: St. Jude's Ranch for Children, 100 St. Jude's St., Boulder City, NV 89005-1618. Those wishing to buy Born Again Cards can send $6.50 for a package of 10 to the ranch at P. O. Box 60100, Boulder City, NV 89006-0100. Use the same address for any other correspondence. For credit card purchases, call (800) 492-3562. For other information, call (702) 294-7124.

December 25

Los Medicos Voladores (LMV):
Los Medicos Voladores (LMV), also
known as the "Flying Doctors," was
founded in 1974 to provide health
services and education to the people of
northern Mexico. LMV's primary
purpose is to send medical teams on 4-
day trips to Mexico each month. Teams
include a pilot, translator, medical

professional (usually medical doctor, dentist, optometrist or chiropractor) and possibly a co-pilot or general volunteer. Donations from individuals, companies and service organizations help members purchase medical, dental and health care supplies, clinic and communications equipment. For more information about volunteering or where to donate equipment, supplies or money, call Los Medicos Voladores at (800) 585-4LMV.